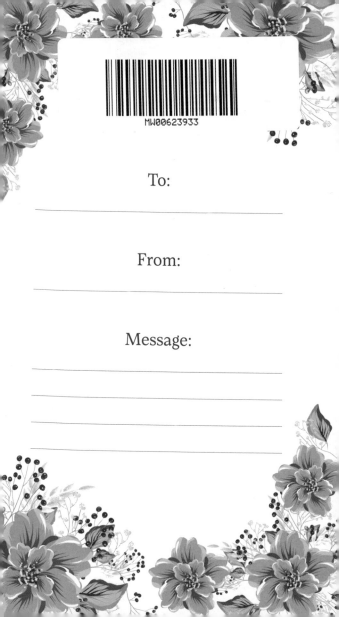

MW00623933

To:

From:

Message:

Published by Christian Art Publishers
PO Box 1599, Vereeniging, 1930, RSA

© 2007
First edition 2007
Second edition 2015
Third edition 2024

Originally published under the title
Becoming A Woman of Worth Promise Book

Designed by Christian Art Publishers
Cover designed by Christian Art Publishers
Images used under license from Shutterstock.com

Printed in China

ISBN 978-0-638-00164-8

24 25 26 27 28 29 30 31 32 33 – 11 10 9 8 7 6 5 4 3 2

PROMISES
from the
WORD
for *Women*

CHRISTIAN ART
PUBLISHERS

Introduction

Do you know that you are a woman of great worth? God designed you with a special purpose and plan.

To God you are more precious than rubies and the Scripture verses in this book will help you to live as the rare jewel that you are in the Father's royal diadem.

You will find encouragement and inspiration as you strive to shine and reflect the Father's love and light to all around you.

May God's richest blessings be upon you as you seek to become the woman God wants you to be.

Contents

As a woman of worth...

Wait on the Lord

Live in such a way that God's love
can bless you as you wait for the eternal
life that our Lord Jesus Christ
in His mercy is going to give you.

Jude 21 NLT

Those who hope in the Lord will renew
their strength. They will soar on wings
like eagles; they will run and not grow
weary, they will walk and not be faint.

Isaiah 40:31 NIV

But for You, O Lord, do I wait;
it is You, O Lord my God,
who will answer.

Psalm 38:15 ESV

We have come to share in Christ,
if indeed we hold our original
conviction firmly to the very end.

Hebrews 3:14 NIV

Hope in the LORD and keep His way.
He will exalt you to inherit the land.

Psalm 37:34 NIV

No one has heard, no ear has perceived,
no eye has seen any God besides You,
who acts on behalf of those
who wait for Him.

Isaiah 64:4 NIV

Our soul waits for the LORD;
He is our help and our shield.

Psalm 33:20 NKJV

Walk in God's Ways

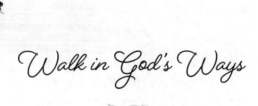

Walk in obedience to all that
the LORD your God has commanded you,
so that you may live and prosper
and prolong your days in the
land that you will possess.

Deuteronomy 5:33 NIV

"The LORD will establish you
as a holy people to Himself,
just as He has sworn to you,
if you keep the commandments
of the LORD your God
and walk in His ways."

Deuteronomy 28:9 NKJV

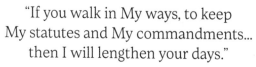

"If you walk in My ways, to keep
My statutes and My commandments...
then I will lengthen your days."

1 Kings 3:14 NKJV

Those who walk uprightly
enter into peace; they find rest.

Isaiah 57:2 NIV

If we walk in the light, as He is
in the light, we have fellowship
with one another, and the
blood of Jesus, His Son,
purifies us from all sin.

1 John 1:7 NIV

"Stand in the ways and see,
and ask for the old paths,
where the good way is, and walk in it;
then you will find rest for your souls."

Jeremiah 6:16 NKJV

Be Watchful

I watch in hope for the LORD,
I wait for God my Savior;
my God will hear me.

Micah 7:7 NIV

She watches over
the affairs of her household...
A woman who fears the LORD
is to be praised. Honor her for
all that her hands have done,
and let her works bring her praise.

Proverbs 31:27, 30-31 NIV

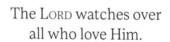

The Lord watches over
all who love Him.

Psalm 145:20 NIV

Be careful!
Watch out for attacks from
the devil, your great enemy.
He prowls around like a roaring lion,
looking for some victim to devour.

1 Peter 5:8 NLT

"I will instruct you and
teach you in the way you
should go; I will counsel you
with My loving eye on you."

Psalm 32:8 NIV

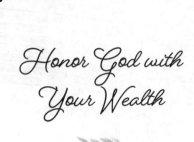

Honor God with Your Wealth

As for the rich in this present age,
charge them not to be haughty,
nor to set their hopes on the uncertainty
of riches, but on God, who richly provides
us with everything to enjoy. They are
to do good, to be rich in good works,
to be generous and ready to share.

1 Timothy 6:17-18 ESV

Remember the LORD your God,
for it is He who gives you the ability
to produce wealth, and so confirms
His covenant, which He swore to
your ancestors, as it is today.

Deuteronomy 8:18 NIV

"Don't store up treasures here on earth, where they can be eaten by moths and get rusty, and where thieves break in and steal. Store your treasures in heaven, where they will never become moth-eaten or rusty and where they will be safe from thieves."

Matthew 6:19-20 NLT

Day by day the LORD takes care of the innocent, and they will receive a reward that lasts forever. They will survive through hard times; even in famine they will have more than enough.

Psalm 37:18-19 NLT

Honor the LORD with your wealth and with the best part of everything your land produces. Then He will fill your barns with grain, and your vats will overflow with the finest wine.

Proverbs 3:9-10 NLT

Live Wholeheartedly

Trust in the LORD with
all your heart and lean not
on your own understanding;
in all your ways submit to Him,
and He will make your paths straight.

Proverbs 3:5-6 NIV

Whatever you do,
work at it with all your heart,
as working for the Lord, not
for human masters.

Colossians 3:23 NIV

But if from there you seek
the LORD your God, you will find
Him if you seek Him with all
your heart and with all your soul.

Deuteronomy 4:29 NIV

Therefore, I urge you, brothers and
sisters, in view of God's mercy, to
offer your bodies as a living sacrifice,
holy and pleasing to God—this is
your true and proper worship.

Romans 12:1 NIV

"Whom shall I send, and who
will go for us?" Then I said,
"Here am I! Send me."

Isaiah 6:8 NKJV

Be Willing to Serve

"If you try to keep your life for yourself,
you will lose it. But if you give up your life
for Me, you will find true life."

Matthew 16:25 NLT

Serve wholeheartedly, as if you were
serving the Lord, not people,
because you know that
the Lord will reward each one
for whatever good they do.

Ephesians 6:7-8 NIV

Fear the LORD, and serve Him in truth
with all your heart; for consider what
great things He has done for you.

1 Samuel 12:24 NKJV

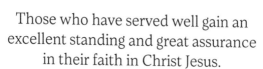

Those who have served well gain an excellent standing and great assurance in their faith in Christ Jesus.

1 Timothy 3:13 NIV

"Whoever would be great among you must be your servant, and whoever would be first among you must be your slave, even as the Son of Man came not to be served but to serve."

Matthew 20:26-28 ESV

"My Father will honor the one who serves Me."

John 12:26 NIV

Run to Win

I press on toward the goal
to win the prize for which God
has called me heavenward
in Christ Jesus.

Philippians 3:14 NIV

Despite all these things,
overwhelming victory is ours
through Christ, who loved us.

Romans 8:37 NLT

How we thank God, who gives
us victory over sin and death through
Jesus Christ our Lord!

1 Corinthians 15:57 NLT

Remember that in a race everyone runs, but only one person gets the prize. You also must run in such a way that you will win. I run straight to the goal with purpose in every step. I discipline my body like an athlete, training it to do what it should. Otherwise, I fear that after preaching to others I myself might be disqualified.

1 Corinthians 9:24, 26-27 NLT

Who is it that overcomes the world except the one who believes that Jesus is the Son of God?

1 John 5:5 ESV

Pursue Wisdom

I keep asking that the God of our
Lord Jesus Christ, the glorious Father,
may give you the Spirit of
wisdom and revelation, so that
you may know Him better.

Ephesians 1:17 NIV

If you need wisdom—if you want to know
what God wants you to do—ask Him,
and He will gladly tell you.

James 1:5 NLT

Wisdom is like honey for you:
if you find it, there is a future hope for
you, and your hope will not be cut off.

Proverbs 24:14 NIV

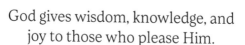

God gives wisdom, knowledge, and
joy to those who please Him.

Ecclesiastes 2:26 NLT

Wisdom is a good thing and
benefits those who see the sun.
Wisdom preserves those who have it.

Ecclesiastes 7:11-12 NIV

"I will give you words and wisdom
that none of your adversaries will
be able to resist or contradict."

Luke 21:15 NIV

Blessed is the one who finds wisdom,
and the one who gets understanding.

Proverbs 3:13 ESV

Bear Witness of Your Faith

We are Christ's ambassadors,
and God is using us to speak
to you. We urge you,
as though Christ Himself
were here pleading with you,
"Be reconciled to God!"

2 Corinthians 5:20 NLT

Then Jesus came to them and said,
"Go and make disciples of all nations,
baptizing them in the name of
the Father and of the Son and of the
Holy Spirit, and teaching them to obey
everything I have commanded you."

Matthew 28:18-20 NIV

"If anyone acknowledges Me publicly here on earth, I, the Son of Man, will openly acknowledge that person in the presence of God's angels."

Luke 12:8 NLT

"Go into all the world and preach the gospel to all creation. Whoever believes and is baptized will be saved."

Mark 16:15-16 NIV

How then shall they call on Him in whom they have not believed? And how shall they believe in Him of whom they have not heard? And how shall they hear without a preacher? And how shall they preach unless they are sent? As it is written: "How beautiful are the feet of those who preach the gospel of peace, who bring glad tidings of good things!"

Romans 10:14-15 NKJV

Know that You Are a Woman of Worth

And now, my daughter, don't be afraid.
I will do for you all you ask.
All the people of my town know that
you are a woman of noble character.

Ruth 3:11 NIV

She is clothed with strength
and dignity, and she laughs with
no fear of the future. When she speaks,
her words are wise, and kindness is
the rule when she gives instructions.

Proverbs 31:25-26 NLT

A kindhearted
woman gains honor.

Proverbs 11:16 NIV

And the LORD God said,
"It is not good for the man
to be alone. I will make a
companion who will help him."

Genesis 2:18 NLT

Beauty should not come from
outward adornment. Rather, it should
be that of your inner self, the unfading
beauty of a gentle and quiet spirit,
which is of great worth in God's sight.

1 Peter 3:3-4 NIV

Work Willingly

Commit to the L ORD whatever you do,
and He will establish your plans.

Proverbs 16:3 NIV

In all toil there is profit,
but mere talk tends only to poverty.

Proverbs 14:23 ESV

Be strong and steady,
always enthusiastic about
the Lord's work, for you know
that nothing you do for the
Lord is ever useless.

1 Corinthians 15:58 NLT

The hand of the diligent will rule.
Proverbs 12:24 NKJV

We always thank God
for all of you and continually
mention you in our prayers.
We remember before our God
and Father your work produced
by faith, your labor prompted
by love, and your endurance inspired
by hope in our Lord Jesus Christ.
1 Thessalonians 1:2-3 NIV

You will enjoy the fruit of your labor.
How happy you will be!
How rich your life!
Psalm 128:2 NLT

Worship Wholeheartedly

Since we are receiving a kingdom
that cannot be shaken, let us be
thankful, and so worship God
acceptably with reverence and awe.

Hebrews 12:28 NIV

It is good to give thanks to the LORD,
to sing praises to Your name,
O Most High; to declare
Your steadfast love in the morning,
and Your faithfulness by night.

Psalm 92:1-2 ESV

"Worship the LORD your God;
it is He who will deliver you from
the hand of all your enemies."

2 Kings 17:39 NIV

Worship the LORD with gladness;
come before Him with joyful songs.

Psalm 100:2 NIV

Great is the LORD! He is most
worthy of praise! He is to be
revered above all the gods.

Psalm 96:4 NLT

Rejoice in the Lord always. Again I
will say, rejoice! Let your gentleness
be known to all men. The Lord is at
hand. Be anxious for nothing, but in
everything by prayer and supplication,
with thanksgiving, let your requests
be made known to God; and the
peace of God, which surpasses all
understanding, will guard your hearts
and minds through Christ Jesus.

Philippians 4:4-7 NKJV

Accept Your Worth

Behold what manner of love the
Father has bestowed on us, that we
should be called children of God!

1 John 3:1 NKJV

I praise You because I am fearfully and
wonderfully made; Your works are
wonderful, I know that full well.

Psalm 139:14 NIV

We are God's masterpiece.

Ephesians 2:10 NLT

You are a chosen generation, a royal
priesthood, a holy nation, His own
special people, that you may proclaim
the praises of Him who called you out
of darkness into His marvelous light.

1 Peter 2:9 NKJV

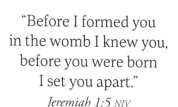

"Before I formed you
in the womb I knew you,
before you were born
I set you apart."
Jeremiah 1:5 NIV

"For I know the plans I have for you,"
declares the LORD, "plans to prosper
you and not to harm you, plans to
give you hope and a future."
Jeremiah 29:11 NIV

And we all, with unveiled face, beholding
the glory of the Lord, are being
transformed into the same image from
one degree of glory to another. For this
comes from the Lord who is the Spirit.
2 Corinthians 3:18 ESV

Obey God's Word

"Obey Me, and I will be
your God and you will be My people.
Walk in obedience to all I command you,
that it may go well with you."

Jeremiah 7:23 NIV

"If you love Me, keep My commands...
Whoever has My commands and
keeps them is the one who loves Me.
The one who loves Me will be loved
by My Father, and I too will love
them and show Myself to them."

John 14:15, 21 NIV

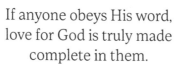

If anyone obeys His word,
love for God is truly made
complete in them.

1 John 2:5 NIV

"If you walk in My ways, to keep
My statutes and My commandments,
as your father David walked,
then I will lengthen your days."

1 Kings 3:14 NKJV

"Not everyone who says to Me,
'Lord, Lord,' will enter the kingdom
of heaven, but only the one who does
the will of My Father who is in heaven."

Matthew 7:21 NIV

Set Godly Objectives

I press on to take hold of that for
which Christ Jesus took hold of me.
I press on toward the goal to win
the prize for which God has called
me heavenward in Christ Jesus.

Philippians 3:12, 14 NIV

I eagerly expect and hope that
I will in no way be ashamed,
but will have sufficient courage
so that now as always Christ will
be exalted in my body, whether
by life or by death. For to me,
to live is Christ and to die is gain.

Philippians 1:20-21 NIV

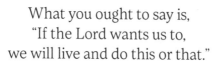

What you ought to say is,
"If the Lord wants us to,
we will live and do this or that."

James 4:15 NLT

Yet indeed I also count all things
loss for the excellence of the knowledge
of Christ Jesus my Lord, for whom I have
suffered the loss of all things, and count
them as rubbish, that I may gain Christ
and be found in Him, not having my own
righteousness, which is from the law,
but that which is through faith
in Christ, the righteousness
which is from God by faith.

Philippians 3:8-9 NKJV

"But for this purpose I have raised you up,
to show you My power, so that My name
may be proclaimed in all the earth."

Exodus 9:16 ESV

Be Observant

Consider the blameless,
observe the upright; a future
awaits those who seek peace.

Psalm 37:37 NIV

I applied my heart to what I observed
and learned a lesson from what I saw.

Proverbs 24:32 NIV

You are my strength, I watch for You;
You, God, are my fortress, my God on
whom I can rely. God will go before me.

Psalm 59:9-10 NIV

"And you shall know the truth,
and the truth shall make you free."

John 8:32 NKJV

Happy are those who listen to me,
watching for me daily at my gates,
waiting for me outside my home!
For whoever finds me finds life
and wins approval from the LORD.
But those who miss me have
injured themselves.

Proverbs 8:34-36 NLT

Watch out that you do not
lose what we have worked for,
but that you may be rewarded fully.

2 John 8 NIV

Offer Freely

Let each one give as he purposes in
his heart, not grudgingly or of necessity;
for God loves a cheerful giver.

2 Corinthians 9:7 NKJV

May He remember all your sacrifices
and accept your burnt offerings.
May He give you the desire of your
heart and make all your plans succeed.

Psalm 20:3-4 NIV

"This poor widow has given more
than all the rest of them.
For they have given a tiny part
of their surplus, but she, poor as she is,
has given everything she has."

Luke 21:3-4 NLT

"Bring the full tithe into the storehouse,
that there may be food in My house.
And thereby put Me to the test,
says the LORD of hosts, if I will not
open the windows of heaven for you
and pour down for you a blessing
until there is no more need."

Malachi 3:10 ESV

Offer your bodies as a living sacrifice,
holy and pleasing to God—this is
your true and proper worship. Do not
conform to the pattern of this world,
but be transformed by the renewing
of your mind. Then you will be able to
test and approve what God's will is—
His good, pleasing and perfect will.

Romans 12:1-2 NIV

Cherish Your Children

He took a child and put him in the midst
of them, and taking him in His arms,
He said to them, "Whoever receives
one such child in My name receives
Me, and whoever receives Me, receives
not Me but Him who sent Me."

Mark 9:36-37 ESV

Train up a child in the way he
should go, and when he is old
he will not depart from it.

Proverbs 22:6 NKJV

Who can find a virtuous wife?
For her worth is far above rubies...
Her children rise up and call her blessed;
her husband also, and he praises her.

Proverbs 31:10, 28 NKJV

Children's children are a crown
to the aged, and parents are
the pride of their children.

Proverbs 17:6 NIV

Once I was young, and now I am old.
Yet I have never seen the godly forsaken,
nor seen their children begging for bread.
The godly always give generous loans to
others, and their children are a blessing.

Psalm 37:25-26 NLT

All your children shall be taught
by the LORD, and great shall be
the peace of your children.

Isaiah 54:13 ESV

Be Open-Handed

As each one has received a gift,
minister it to one another, as good
stewards of the manifold grace of God.

1 Peter 4:10 NKJV

Good will come to those who
are generous and lend freely,
who conduct their affairs with justice.
Surely the righteous will never be shaken;
they will be remembered forever.

Psalm 112:5-6 NIV

If you help the poor,
you are lending to the LORD—
and He will repay you!

Proverbs 19:17 NLT

You will be enriched so that
you can give even more generously.
And when we take your gifts to those
who need them, they will break
out in thanksgiving to God.

2 Corinthians 9:11 NLT

Let them do good, that they be
rich in good works, ready to give,
willing to share, storing up for
themselves a good foundation
for the time to come, that they
may lay hold on eternal life.

1 Timothy 6:18-19 NKJV

Be Open-Hearted

May the Lord make your love
grow and overflow to each other
and to everyone else, just as our
love overflows toward you.

1 Thessalonians 3:12 NLT

"Love your enemies, do good to them,
and lend to them without expecting
to get anything back. Then your reward
will be great, and you will be children of
the Most High, because He is kind to
the ungrateful and wicked. Be merciful,
just as your Father is merciful."

Luke 6:35-36 NIV

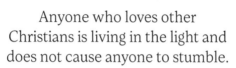

Anyone who loves other
Christians is living in the light and
does not cause anyone to stumble.

1 John 2:10 NLT

For this very reason, make every effort
to add to your faith goodness...
and to godliness, mutual affection;
and to mutual affection, love. For if you
possess these qualities in increasing
measure, they will keep you from being
ineffective and unproductive in your
knowledge of our Lord Jesus Christ.

2 Peter 1:5, 7-8 NIV

No one has ever seen God;
if we love one another, God abides
in us and His love is perfected in us.

1 John 4:12 ESV

Always Be Optimistic

A cheerful look brings joy to the heart;
good news makes for good health.

Proverbs 15:30 NLT

I have learned the secret of living in
every situation, whether it is with a full
stomach or empty, with plenty or little.
For I can do everything with the help of
Christ who gives me the strength I need.

Philippians 4:12-13 NLT

I remain confident of this:
I will see the goodness of the
Lord in the land of the living.
Wait for the Lord; be strong and
take heart and wait for the Lord.

Psalm 27:13-14 NIV

This is the confidence that we
have in Him, that if we ask anything
according to His will, He hears us.

1 John 5:14 NKJV

Praise be to the God and Father of
our Lord Jesus Christ! In His great
mercy He has given us new birth
into a living hope through the
resurrection of Jesus Christ from
the dead, and into an inheritance
that can never perish, spoil or fade.
This inheritance is kept in heaven for you.

1 Peter 1:3-4 NIV

So we may boldly say,
"The LORD is my helper;
I will not fear. What can
man do to me?"

Hebrews 13:6 NKJV

Organize Your Life

An excellent wife who can find?
She is far more precious than jewels.
She rises while it is yet night
and provides food for her household.
She considers a field and buys it;
with the fruit of her hands
she plants a vineyard.

Proverbs 31:10, 15-16 ESV

Commit your work to the LORD,
and then your plans will succeed.

Proverbs 16:3 NLT

Good planning and
hard work lead to prosperity,
but hasty shortcuts lead to poverty.

Proverbs 21:5 NLT

Those who plan what is
good find love and faithfulness.

Proverbs 14:22 NIV

She looks well to the ways of
her household and does not
eat the bread of idleness.

Proverbs 31:27 ESV

The plans of the diligent
lead to profit as surely as
haste leads to poverty.

Proverbs 21:5 NIV

Overcome the Odds

We can rejoice when we run into
problems and trials, for we know
that they are good for us—they help
us learn to endure. And endurance
develops strength of character in
us, and character strengthens our
confident expectation of salvation.

Romans 5:3-4 NLT

"To the one who is victorious,
I will give the right to eat from
the tree of life, which is
in the paradise of God."

Revelation 2:7 NIV

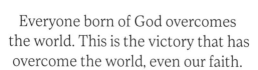

Everyone born of God overcomes
the world. This is the victory that has
overcome the world, even our faith.

1 John 5:4 NIV

"The one who conquers will be clothed
thus in white garments, and I will
never blot his name out of the book
of life. I will confess his name before
my Father and before His angels."

Revelation 3:5 ESV

Do not be overcome by evil,
but overcome evil with good.

Romans 12:21 NIV

Patient endurance
leads to godliness.

2 Peter 1:6 NLT

Overlook Wrongs

Hatred stirs up strife,
but love covers all sins.

Proverbs 10:12 NKJV

"Judge not, that you be not judged.
For with the judgment you pronounce
you will be judged, and with the measure
you use it will be measured to you.
Why do you see the speck that is in
your brother's eye, but do not notice
the log that is in your own eye?"

Matthew 7:1-3 ESV

Be kind and compassionate
to one another, forgiving each other,
just as in Christ God forgave you.

Ephesians 4:32 NIV

Bear with each other and forgive
one another if any of you has
a grievance against someone.
Forgive as the Lord forgave you.

Colossians 3:13 NIV

"If you forgive those who sin against you,
your heavenly Father will forgive you.
But if you refuse to forgive others,
your Father will not forgive your sins."

Matthew 6:14-15 NLT

Most important of all, continue to
show deep love for each other,
for love covers a multitude of sins.

1 Peter 4:8 NLT

Own Up

If we confess our sins to Him,
He is faithful and just to forgive us
and to cleanse us from every wrong.

1 John 1:9 NLT

Whoever conceals his transgressions
will not prosper, but he who confesses
and forsakes them will obtain mercy.

Proverbs 28:13 ESV

"Come now, let us settle the matter,"
says the LORD. "Though your sins are
like scarlet, they shall be as white
as snow; though they are red as
crimson, they shall be like wool."

Isaiah 1:18 NIV

When Jesus saw their faith, He said
to the paralytic, "Son, be of good cheer;
your sins are forgiven you."

Matthew 9:2 NKJV

What joy for those whose record
the LORD has cleared of sin, whose
lives are lived in complete honesty.

Psalm 32:2 NLT

The path of the righteous is like
the light of dawn, which shines
brighter and brighter until full day.

Proverbs 4:18 ESV

Know that You Are Radiant

You have turned for me my mourning
into dancing; You have loosed my
sackcloth and clothed me with gladness,
that my glory may sing Your praise
and not be silent. O LORD my God,
I will give thanks to You forever!

Psalm 30:11-12 ESV

Moses was not aware that
his face was radiant because
he had spoken with the LORD.

Exodus 34:29 NIV

Light shines on the righteous
and joy on the upright in heart.

Psalm 97:11 NIV

Blessed are the people who know
the festal shout, who walk, O LORD,
in the light of Your face, who exult
in Your name all the day and in
Your righteousness are exalted.
For You are the glory of their strength;
by Your favor our horn is exalted.

Psalm 89:15-17 ESV

All of us have had that veil removed
so that we can be mirrors that brightly
reflect the glory of the Lord. And as the
Spirit of the Lord works within us,
we become more and more like Him
and reflect His glory even more.

2 Corinthians 3:18 NLT

Know that You Are Rare

"My dove, my perfect one, is unique,
the only daughter of her mother,
the favorite of the one who bore her."

Song of Songs 6:9 NIV

"I will not forget you!
See, I have engraved you
on the palms of My hands."

Isaiah 49:15-16 NIV

"You have been set apart as holy to the
LORD your God, and He has chosen
you to be His own special treasure
from all the nations of the earth."

Deuteronomy 14:2 NLT

"Because you are precious in My eyes,
and honored, and I love you,
I give men in return for you,
peoples in exchange for your life."

Isaiah 43:4 ESV

"You yourselves have seen how
I bore you on eagles' wings
and brought you to Myself.
Now therefore, if you will indeed
obey My voice and keep
My covenant, you shall be
My treasured possession among
all peoples, for all the earth is Mine."

Exodus 19:4-5 ESV

Be Reasonable

"I will give you a wise and discerning heart, so that there will never have been anyone like you, nor will there ever be."

1 Kings 3:12 NIV

"The fear of the LORD is the beginning of wisdom, and the knowledge of the Holy One is understanding."

Proverbs 9:10 NKJV

You will keep in perfect peace all who trust in You, whose thoughts are fixed on You.

Isaiah 26:3 NLT

To acquire wisdom
is to love oneself;
people who cherish
understanding will prosper.

Proverbs 19:8 NLT

People with understanding
control their anger; a hot temper
shows great foolishness.

Proverbs 14:29 NLT

People ruin their lives by their
own foolishness and then are
angry at the LORD.

Proverbs 19:3 NLT

Take Time to Reflect

I have more understanding
than all my teachers, for Your
testimonies are my meditation.
Psalm 119:99 NKJV

Reflect on what I am saying,
for the Lord will give you insight
into all of this.
2 Timothy 2:7 NIV

Fix your thoughts on Jesus,
whom we acknowledge as
our apostle and high priest.
Hebrews 3:1 NIV

So I reflected on all this and concluded
that the righteous and the wise and what
they do are in God's hands, but no one
knows whether love or hate awaits them.

Ecclesiastes 9:1 NIV

Fix your thoughts on what is
true and honorable and right.
Think about things that are pure and
lovely and admirable. Think about things
that are excellent and worthy of praise.

Philippians 4:8 NLT

I remember the days of old.
I ponder all Your great works.
I think about what You have done.

Psalm 143:5 NLT

Rejoice Always

"Rejoice and be exceedingly glad,
for great is your reward in heaven."
Matthew 5:12 NKJV

Let all who take refuge in You
be glad; let them ever sing for joy.
Spread Your protection over them,
that those who love Your name may
rejoice in You. Surely, LORD, You bless
the righteous; You surround them
with Your favor as with a shield.
Psalm 5:11-12 NIV

Rejoice to the extent that you
partake of Christ's sufferings,
that when His glory is revealed,
you may also be glad with exceeding joy.
1 Peter 4:13 NKJV

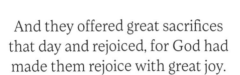

And they offered great sacrifices
that day and rejoiced, for God had
made them rejoice with great joy.

Nehemiah 12:43 ESV

The godly will rejoice in the LORD
and find shelter in Him. And those
who do what is right will praise Him.

Psalm 64:10 NLT

I trust in Your unfailing love.
I will rejoice because You have
rescued me. I will sing to the LORD
because He has been so good to me.

Psalm 13:5-6 NLT

Repent of Wrongs

"In repentance and rest is your salvation,
in quietness and trust is your strength."

Isaiah 30:15 NIV

The Lord is not slow in keeping
His promise, as some understand
slowness. Instead He is patient
with you, not wanting anyone to perish,
but everyone to come to repentance.

2 Peter 3:9 NIV

God can use sorrow in our lives to help
us turn away from sin and seek salvation.
We will never regret that kind of sorrow.

2 Corinthians 7:10 NLT

"If you return to Me, I will restore you
so you can continue to serve Me."

Jeremiah 15:19 NLT

If we confess our sins, He is faithful
and just to forgive us our sins and to
cleanse us from all unrighteousness.

1 John 1:9 NKJV

"I say to you, there is joy in the
presence of the angels of God
over one sinner who repents."

Luke 15:10 NKJV

Repent therefore, and turn back,
that your sins may be blotted out.

Acts 3:19 ESV

Respect Others

"My covenant was with him, a covenant
of life and peace, and I gave them to him;
this called for reverence and he revered
Me and stood in awe of My name."

Malachi 2:5 NIV

Love each other with
genuine affection, and take
delight in honoring each other.

Romans 12:10 NLT

A kindhearted woman gains honor.

Proverbs 11:16 NIV

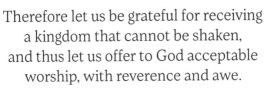

Therefore let us be grateful for receiving
a kingdom that cannot be shaken,
and thus let us offer to God acceptable
worship, with reverence and awe.

Hebrews 12:28 ESV

"So whatever you wish that others
would do to you, do also to them."

Matthew 7:12 ESV

"Show your fear of God by
standing up in the presence of
elderly people and showing respect
for the aged. I am the LORD."

Leviticus 19:32 NLT

Be Responsible

"To those who use well what
they are given, even more will be given,
and they will have an abundance."

Matthew 25:29 NLT

Have confidence in your leaders and
submit to their authority, because they
keep watch over you as those who
must give an account. Do this so that
their work will be a joy, not a burden,
for that would be of no benefit to you.

Hebrews 13:17 NIV

If God has given you leadership ability,
take the responsibility seriously.

Romans 12:8 NLT

The wise woman builds her house,
but with her own hands the
foolish one tears hers down.

Proverbs 14:1 NIV

You have given him dominion
over the works of Your hands;
You have put all things under
his feet, all sheep and oxen,
and also the beasts of the field.

Psalm 8:6-7 ESV

Know that You Are Rich

A faithful man will abound
with blessings, but whoever hastens
to be rich will not go unpunished.

Proverbs 28:20 ESV

Hasn't God chosen the poor in this
world to be rich in faith? Aren't they
the ones who will inherit the kingdom
God promised to those who love Him?

James 2:5 NLT

Happy are those who fear the LORD.
Yes, happy are those who delight
in doing what He commands.
They themselves will be wealthy,
and their good deeds
will never be forgotten.

Psalm 112:1, 3 NLT

You will be enriched in every way so
that you can be generous on every
occasion, and through us your generosity
will result in thanksgiving to God.

2 Corinthians 9:11 NIV

You are a chosen generation,
a royal priesthood, a holy nation,
His own special people, that you
may proclaim the praises of Him
who called you out of darkness
into His marvelous light.

1 Peter 2:9 NKJV

What are mortals that You should
think of us, mere humans that You
should care for us? For You made us
only a little lower than God, and You
crowned us with glory and honor.

Psalm 8:4-5 NLT

Pursue Righteousness

The righteous cry out, and the LORD hears,
and delivers them out of all their troubles.

Psalm 34:17 NKJV

And now the prize awaits me—
the crown of righteousness that the Lord,
the righteous Judge, will give me on that
great day of His return. And the prize is
not just for me but for all who eagerly
look forward to His glorious return.

2 Timothy 4:8 NLT

But the path of the righteous is like
the light of dawn, which shines
brighter and brighter until full day.

Proverbs 4:18 ESV

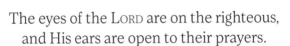

The eyes of the LORD are on the righteous,
and His ears are open to their prayers.

1 Peter 3:12 NKJV

When the kindness and love of God
our Savior appeared, He saved us,
not because of righteous things we
had done, but because of His mercy.
He saved us through the washing of
rebirth and renewal by the Holy Spirit.

Titus 3:4-5 NIV

"The righteous will shine like the
sun in the kingdom of their Father."

Matthew 13:43 NIV

Stay Firmly Rooted

Just as you accepted Christ Jesus as your Lord, you must continue to live in obedience to Him. Let your roots grow down into Him and draw up nourishment from Him, so you will grow in faith, strong and vigorous in the truth you were taught.

Colossians 2:6-7 NLT

"I have called you by your name; you are Mine. You have been honored, and I have loved you."

Isaiah 43:1, 4 NKJV

Fixing our eyes on Jesus, the pioneer and perfecter of faith. For the joy set before Him He endured the cross, scorning its shame, and sat down at the right hand of the throne of God.

Hebrews 12:2 NIV

Blessed are those who trust in the LORD and have made the LORD their hope and confidence. They are like trees planted along a riverbank, with roots that reach deep into the water. Such trees are not bothered by the heat or worried by long months of drought. Their leaves stay green, and they go right on producing delicious fruit.

Jeremiah 17:7-8 NLT

According to the grace of God which was given to me, as a wise master builder I have laid the foundation, and another builds on it. But let each one take heed how he builds on it. For no other foundation can anyone lay than that which is laid, which is Jesus Christ.

1 Corinthians 3:10-11 NKJV

Practice Tact

Be of one mind, having compassion
for one another; love as brothers,
be tenderhearted, be courteous;
not returning evil for evil or reviling for
reviling, but on the contrary blessing.

1 Peter 3:8-9 NKJV

"For the mouth speaks what the heart
is full of. A good man brings good things
out of the good stored up in him, and
an evil man brings evil things out of
the evil stored up in him. For by your
words you will be acquitted, and by
your words you will be condemned."

Matthew 12:34-35, 37 NIV

If you shout a pleasant greeting to
your neighbor too early in the morning,
it will be counted as a curse!

Proverbs 27:14 NLT

Kind words are like honey—sweet to
the soul and healthy for the body.

Proverbs 16:24 NLT

Words satisfy the soul as food
satisfies the stomach; the right words
on a person's lips bring satisfaction.

Proverbs 18:20 NLT

"The Lord God has given me
the tongue of those who are taught,
that I may know how to sustain
with a word him who is weary."

Isaiah 50:4 ESV

There is one whose rash words
are like sword thrusts, but the
tongue of the wise brings healing.

Proverbs 12:18 ESV

Use Your Talents

To each is given the manifestation
of the Spirit for the common good.

1 Corinthians 12:7 ESV

Since you are so eager to have
spiritual gifts, ask God for those that
will be of real help to the whole church.

1 Corinthians 14:12 NLT

We have different gifts, according to
the grace given to each of us. If your
gift is prophesying, then prophesy
in accordance with your faith; if it is
serving, then serve; if it is teaching,
then teach; if it is to encourage, then give
encouragement; if it is giving, then give
generously; if it is to lead, do it diligently;
if it is to show mercy, do it cheerfully.

Romans 12:6-8 NIV

Each of you should use whatever gift
you have received to serve others,
as faithful stewards of God's grace in
its various forms. If anyone speaks,
they should do so as one who speaks
the very words of God. If anyone serves,
they should do so with the strength
God provides, so that in all things God
may be praised through Jesus Christ.

1 Peter 4:10-11 NIV

How we praise God, the Father of
our Lord Jesus Christ, who has
blessed us with every spiritual
blessing in the heavenly realms
because we belong to Christ.

Ephesians 1:3 NLT

Teach Your Children

Teach your children to choose
the right path, and when they are older,
they will remain upon it.

Proverbs 22:6 NLT

"Do not worry about how you will
defend yourselves or what you will say,
for the Holy Spirit will teach you at
that time what you should say."

Luke 12:11-12 NIV

My child, listen when your father
corrects you. Don't neglect your mother's
instruction. What you learn from them
will crown you with grace and be a
chain of honor around your neck.

Proverbs 1:8-9 NLT

To discipline and reprimand a
child produces wisdom, but a mother
is disgraced by an undisciplined child.

Proverbs 29:15 NLT

When she speaks, her words
are wise, and kindness is the rule
when she gives instructions.

Proverbs 31:26 NLT

"You will be able to tell wonderful
stories to your children and
grandchildren about the
marvelous things I am doing."

Exodus 10:2 NLT

Be Tender-Hearted

Be kind to each other, tenderhearted,
forgiving one another, just as God
through Christ has forgiven you.

Ephesians 4:32 NLT

Your own soul is nourished when
you are kind, but you destroy
yourself when you are cruel.

Proverbs 11:17 NLT

Do nothing from selfish ambition or
conceit, but in humility count others
more significant than yourselves.

Philippians 2:3 ESV

"You must be compassionate,
just as your Father is compassionate."

Luke 6:36 NLT

But the fruit of the Spirit is love, joy,
peace, patience, kindness, goodness,
faithfulness, gentleness, self-control.

Galatians 5:22-23 ESV

Finally, all of you should be
of one mind. Sympathize with
each other. Love each other
as brothers and sisters.
Be tenderhearted, and keep
a humble attitude.

1 Peter 3:8 NLT

Be Thankful

Wealth and honor come from You.
In Your hands are strength
and power to exalt and give
strength to all. We give You thanks,
and praise Your glorious name.

1 Chronicles 29:12-13 NIV

I will praise You, for You have answered
me, and have become my salvation.

Psalm 118:21 NKJV

The LORD is my strength, my shield
from every danger. I trust in Him
with all my heart. He helps me,
and my heart is filled with joy.
I burst out in songs of thanksgiving.

Psalm 28:7 NLT

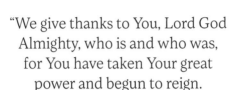

"We give thanks to You, Lord God Almighty, who is and who was, for You have taken Your great power and begun to reign.

Revelation 11:17 ESV

But we ought always to thank God for you, brothers and sisters loved by the Lord, because God chose you as firstfruits to be saved through the sanctifying work of the Spirit and through belief in the truth.

2 Thessalonians 2:13 NIV

Thanks be to God, who gives us the victory through our Lord Jesus Christ.

1 Corinthians 15:57 NKJV

Be Thoughtful

Fix your thoughts on what is true and
honorable and right. Think about things
that are pure and lovely and admirable.
Think about things that are excellent
and worthy of praise.

Philippians 4:8 NLT

"Blessed are the pure in heart,
for they shall see God."

Matthew 5:8 ESV

I am so glad, dear friends,
that you always keep me in your
thoughts and you are following the
Christian teaching I passed on to you.

1 Corinthians 11:2 NLT

I have never stopped thanking
God for you. I pray for you constantly.

Ephesians 1:16 NLT

"So whatever you wish that others
would do to you, do also to them."

Matthew 7:12 ESV

How I praise the Lord that you are
concerned about me again. I know you
have always been concerned for me,
but you didn't have the chance to help
me. Even so, you have done well to
share with me in my present difficulty.

Philippians 4:10, 14 NLT

Be Tolerant

Love is patient and kind.
1 Corinthians 13:4 NLT

A soft answer turns away wrath,
but a harsh word stirs up anger.
Proverbs 15:1 ESV

"Blessed are the merciful,
for they will be shown mercy."
Matthew 5:7 NIV

Finally, all of you, have unity of mind,
sympathy, brotherly love, a tender heart,
and a humble mind. Do not repay evil
for evil or reviling for reviling, but on the
contrary, bless, for to this you were called.
1 Peter 3:8-9 ESV

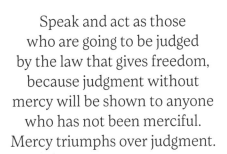

Speak and act as those
who are going to be judged
by the law that gives freedom,
because judgment without
mercy will be shown to anyone
who has not been merciful.
Mercy triumphs over judgment.

James 2:12-13 NIV

Cease from anger, and forsake wrath;
do not fret—it only causes harm.

Psalm 37:8 NKJV

Better a patient person than
a warrior, one with self-control
than one who takes a city.

Proverbs 16:32 NIV

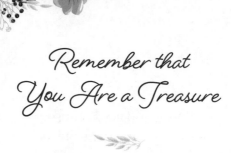

Remember that You Are a Treasure

"If you will indeed obey My voice and keep My covenant, you shall be My treasured possession among all peoples, for all the earth is Mine."

Exodus 19:5 ESV

You made all the delicate, inner parts of my body and knit me together in my mother's womb. Thank You for making me so wonderfully complex! Your workmanship is marvelous—and how well I know it.

Psalm 139:13-14 NLT

"I would not forget you! See, I have written your name on My hand."

Isaiah 49:15-16 NLT

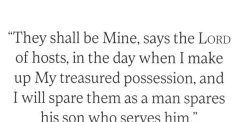

"They shall be Mine, says the Lᴏʀᴅ
of hosts, in the day when I make
up My treasured possession, and
I will spare them as a man spares
his son who serves him."

Malachi 3:17 ᴇsᴠ

The Lᴏʀᴅ has declared today that you
are His people, His own special
treasure, just as He promised.

Deuteronomy 26:18 ɴʟᴛ

"I have called you by your name;
you are Mine. Since you were
precious in My sight, you have
been honored, and I have loved you."

Isaiah 43:1, 4 ɴᴋᴊᴠ

Live Triumphantly

"For the LORD your God is the one who
goes with you to fight for you against
your enemies to give you victory."

Deuteronomy 20:4 NIV

You have given me the shield
of Your salvation, and Your
gentleness made me great.

2 Samuel 22:36 ESV

Every child of God defeats
this evil world by trusting Christ
to give the victory.

1 John 5:4 NLT

He holds success in store for the upright,
He is a shield to those whose walk
is blameless, for He guards the
course of the just and protects
the way of His faithful ones.

Proverbs 2:7-8 NIV

"I have told you all this so that you
may have peace in Me. Here on
earth you will have many trials and
sorrows. But take heart, because
I have overcome the world."

John 16:33 NLT

Be True-Hearted

Whoever speaks the truth
gives honest evidence,
but a false witness utters deceit.

Proverbs 12:17 ESV

Keep a close watch on yourself
and on your teaching. Stay true
to what is right, and God will save
you and those who hear you.

1 Timothy 4:16 NLT

Who may ascend the mountain
of the LORD? Who may stand in
His holy place? The one who has
clean hands and a pure heart.

Psalm 24:3-4 NIV

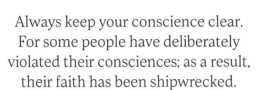

Always keep your conscience clear.
For some people have deliberately
violated their consciences; as a result,
their faith has been shipwrecked.

1 Timothy 1:19 NLT

The truthful lip shall be
established forever, but a lying
tongue is but for a moment.

Proverbs 12:19 NKJV

Trust in the LORD with all your heart
and lean not on your own understanding;
in all your ways submit to Him,
and He will make your paths straight.

Proverbs 3:5-6 NIV

Trust in the Lord

"Blessed are those who trust
in the LORD and have made the LORD
their hope and confidence."

Jeremiah 17:7 NLT

"Behold, God is my salvation;
I will trust, and will not be afraid;
for the LORD GOD is my strength and my
song, and He has become my salvation."

Isaiah 12:2 ESV

Whoever gives thought to the word
will discover good, and blessed
is he who trusts in the LORD.

Proverbs 16:20 ESV

Trust in Him at all times, O people;
pour out your heart before Him;
God is a refuge for us.

Psalm 62:8 ESV

May the God of hope
fill you with all joy and peace
in believing, that you may
abound in hope by the power
of the Holy Spirit.

Romans 15:13 NKJV

Trust in the LORD forever,
for the LORD, the LORD Himself,
is the Rock eternal.

Isaiah 26:4 NIV

Have a Happy Heart

May the righteous be glad
and rejoice before God;
may they be happy and joyful.

Psalm 68:3 NIV

Happy are those who have the
God of Israel as their helper,
whose hope is in the LORD their God.

Psalm 146:5 NLT

Happy are those who fear the LORD.
Yes, happy are those who delight
in doing what He commands.

Psalm 112:1 NLT

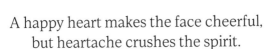

A happy heart makes the face cheerful,
but heartache crushes the spirit.

Proverbs 15:13 NIV

I know the LORD is always with me.
I will not be shaken, for He is right beside
me. No wonder my heart is filled with joy,
and my mouth shouts His praises.

Psalm 16:8-9 NLT

Better is a little with the fear of the LORD
than great treasure and trouble with it.

Proverbs 15:16 ESV

The joy of the LORD is your strength.

Nehemiah 8:10 NLT

Live in Harmony

Live in harmony with one another.
Do not be proud, but be willing to
associate with people of low position.
Do not be conceited. If it is possible,
as far as it depends on you,
live at peace with everyone.

Romans 12:16, 18 NIV

Finally, all of you, be like-minded,
be sympathetic, love one another,
be compassionate and humble.
Do not repay evil with evil or insult
with insult. On the contrary,
repay evil with blessing,
because to this you were called so
that you may inherit a blessing.

1 Peter 3:8-9 NIV

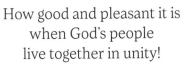

How good and pleasant it is
when God's people
live together in unity!

Psalm 133:1 NIV

May God, who gives this patience
and encouragement, help you live in
complete harmony with each other—
each with the attitude of Christ
Jesus toward the other.

Romans 15:5 NLT

"...so that they may be brought to
complete unity. Then the world will
know that You sent Me and have loved
them even as You have loved Me."

John 17:23 NIV

Nurture a Healthy Heart

If anyone is in Christ,
the new creation has come:
The old has gone, the new is here!

2 Corinthians 5:17 NIV

"Though your sins are like scarlet,
they shall be as white as snow;
though they are red like crimson,
they shall be as wool."

Isaiah 1:18 NKJV

Physical exercise has some value,
but spiritual exercise is much more
important, for it promises a reward
in both this life and the next.

1 Timothy 4:8 NLT

Let us draw near to God
with a sincere heart
and with the full assurance
that faith brings, having our hearts
sprinkled to cleanse us from
a guilty conscience and having
our bodies washed with pure water.

Hebrews 10:22 NIV

Create in me a clean heart, O God,
and renew a steadfast spirit within me.

Psalm 51:10 NKJV

He heals the brokenhearted,
binding up their wounds.

Psalm 147:3 NLT

Be Heavenly-Minded

Our citizenship is in heaven.
And we eagerly await a Savior from
there, the Lord Jesus Christ, who, by
the power that enables Him to bring
everything under His control, will
transform our lowly bodies so that
they will be like His glorious body.

Philippians 3:20-21 NIV

In His great mercy He has given us
new birth into a living hope through
the resurrection of Jesus Christ from
the dead, and into an inheritance that
can never perish, spoil or fade. This
inheritance is kept in heaven for you.

1 Peter 1:3-4 NIV

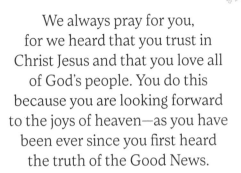

We always pray for you,
for we heard that you trust in
Christ Jesus and that you love all
of God's people. You do this
because you are looking forward
to the joys of heaven—as you have
been ever since you first heard
the truth of the Good News.

Colossians 1:3-5 NLT

We are looking forward
to the new heavens and
new earth He has promised,
a world where everyone
is right with God.

2 Peter 3:13 NLT

"In My Father's house are many
mansions; if it were not so, I would
have told you. I go to prepare a place
for you. And if I go and prepare
a place for you, I will come again
and receive you to Myself."

John 14:2-3 NKJV

Be a Good Helpmate

The Lord God said, "It is not good that man should be alone; I will make him a helper comparable to him." Then the rib which the Lord God had taken from man He made into a woman, and He brought her to the man.

Genesis 2:18, 22 NKJV

Give honor to marriage, and remain faithful to one another in marriage. God will surely judge people who are immoral and those who commit adultery.

Hebrews 13:4 NLT

The wife God gives you is your reward for all your earthly toil.

Ecclesiastes 9:9 NLT

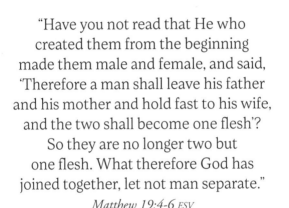

"Have you not read that He who created them from the beginning made them male and female, and said, 'Therefore a man shall leave his father and his mother and hold fast to his wife, and the two shall become one flesh'? So they are no longer two but one flesh. What therefore God has joined together, let not man separate."

Matthew 19:4-6 ESV

Who can find a virtuous and capable wife? She is worth more than precious rubies. Her husband can trust her, and she will greatly enrich his life. She will not hinder him but help him all her life.

Proverbs 31:10-12 NLT

Have a Heroic Heart

"Be strong and courageous.
Do not be afraid; do not be
discouraged, for the LORD your God
will be with you wherever you go."

Joshua 1:9 NIV

Commit everything you do to the LORD.
Trust Him, and He will help you.

Psalm 37:5 NLT

The LORD is my light and
my salvation; whom shall I fear?
The LORD is the strength of my life;
of whom shall I be afraid?

Psalm 27:1 NKJV

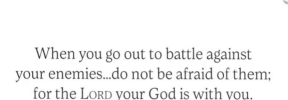

When you go out to battle against
your enemies...do not be afraid of them;
for the LORD your God is with you.

Deuteronomy 20:1 NKJV

Be strong in the Lord
and in His mighty power.

Ephesians 6:10 NIV

"Don't be afraid, for I am with you.
Do not be dismayed, for I am
your God. I will strengthen you.
I will help you. I will uphold you
with My victorious right hand."

Isaiah 41:10 NLT

Pursue Holiness

As He who called you is holy,
you also be holy in all your conduct,
because it is written,
"Be holy, for I am holy."

1 Peter 1:15-16 NKJV

Make every effort to live in peace
with everyone and to be holy;
without holiness no one
will see the Lord.

Hebrews 12:14 NIV

Long ago, even before He made
the world, God loved us and
chose us in Christ to be holy
and without fault in His eyes.

Ephesians 1:4 NLT

I beseech you therefore, by the mercies
of God, that you present your bodies
a living sacrifice, holy, acceptable to
God, which is your reasonable service.

Romans 12:1 NKJV

Your sins have been washed away,
and you have been set apart for God.

1 Corinthians 6:11 NLT

Don't you realize that all of you together
are the temple of God and that the
Spirit of God lives in you? God will
bring ruin upon anyone who ruins
this temple. For God's temple is holy,
and you Christians are that temple.

1 Corinthians 3:16-17 NLT

Make Your Home Blessed

The LORD blesses the
home of the righteous.

Proverbs 3:33 NIV

How happy are those who fear
the LORD. Look at all those children!
There they sit around your table
as vigorous and healthy as
young olive trees.

Psalm 128:1, 3 NLT

Children are a heritage from the LORD,
the fruit of the womb a reward.

Psalm 127:3 ESV

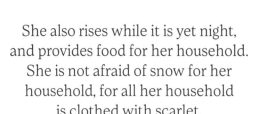

She also rises while it is yet night,
and provides food for her household.
She is not afraid of snow for her
household, for all her household
is clothed with scarlet.

Proverbs 31:15, 21 NKJV

She watches over the ways of
her household, and does not
eat the bread of idleness.

Proverbs 31:27 NKJV

By wisdom a house is built, and
through understanding it is established;
through knowledge its rooms are filled
with rare and beautiful treasures.

Proverbs 24:3-4 NIV

Be Forever Hopeful

May the God of hope fill you with
all joy and peace as you trust in Him,
so that you may overflow with hope
by the power of the Holy Spirit.

Romans 15:13 NIV

Let us hold fast the confession
of our hope without wavering,
for He who promised is faithful.

Hebrews 10:23 NKJV

"For I know the plans I have for
you, declares the LORD, plans for
welfare and not for evil, to give
you a future and a hope."

Jeremiah 29:11 ESV

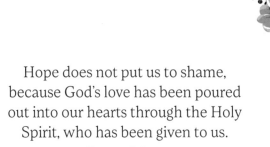

Hope does not put us to shame,
because God's love has been poured
out into our hearts through the Holy
Spirit, who has been given to us.

Romans 5:5 NIV

I wait for the LORD,
my whole being waits,
and in His word I put my hope.

Psalm 130:5 NIV

What is faith? It is the confident
assurance that what we hope for is
going to happen. It is the evidence
of things we cannot yet see.

Hebrews 11:1 NLT

Be Hospitable

Don't forget to show hospitality
to strangers, for some who have
done this have entertained
angels without realizing it!

Hebrews 13:2 NLT

"When you give a feast, invite the poor,
the maimed, the lame, the blind.
And you will be blessed, because they
cannot repay you; for you shall be repaid
at the resurrection of the just."

Luke 14:13-14 NKJV

Offer hospitality to one another
without grumbling. Each of you should
use whatever gift you have received
to serve others, as faithful stewards
of God's grace in its various forms.

1 Peter 4:9-10 NIV

A generous person will prosper;
whoever refreshes others
will be refreshed.

Proverbs 11:25 NIV

You will be enriched so that you
can give even more generously.
And when we take your gifts to
those who need them, they will
break out in thanksgiving to God.

2 Corinthians 9:11 NLT

Command them to do good,
to be rich in good deeds,
and to be generous and willing
to share. In this way they will
lay up treasure for themselves.

1 Timothy 6:18-19 NIV

Practice Humility

The LORD takes pleasure
in His people; He will beautify
the humble with salvation.

Psalm 149:4 NKJV

Humble yourselves in the sight
of the Lord, and He will lift you up.

James 4:10 NKJV

Humble yourselves, therefore, under
the mighty hand of God so that at
the proper time He may exalt you.

1 Peter 5:6 ESV

"For those who exalt themselves will be humbled, and those who humble themselves will be exalted."

Matthew 23:12 NIV

Those who are gentle and lowly will posses the land; they will live in prosperous security.

Psalm 37:11 NLT

Pride leads to disgrace, but with humility comes wisdom.

Proverbs 11:2 NLT

Have a Hunger for God

Oh, how I love Your law!
I meditate on it all day long.
How sweet are Your words to my taste,
sweeter than honey to my mouth!

Psalm 119:97, 103 NIV

The LORD is good to
those who wait for Him,
to the soul who seeks Him.

Lamentations 3:25 ESV

He satisfies the thirsty and
fills the hungry with good things.

Psalm 107:9 NIV

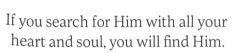

If you search for Him with all your
heart and soul, you will find Him.

Deuteronomy 4:29 NLT

"Ask, and it will be given to you;
seek, and you will find; knock,
and it will be opened to you.
For everyone who asks receives,
and he who seeks finds, and to him
who knocks it will be opened."

Matthew 7:7-8 NKJV

I am fearfully and wonderfully made.

Psalm 139:14 NIV

As the deer pants for streams of water,
so my soul pants for You, O God.
My soul thirsts for God, for the living God.

Psalm 42:1-2 NIV

Charm is deceptive,
and beauty does not last;
but a woman who fears the
LORD will be greatly praised.
Reward her for all she has done.
Let her deeds publicly
declare her praise.

Proverbs 31:30-31 NLT